From Prison to Prosperity

A Convict's Journey to a New Continent

A Play for 5th Year Students

Thomas Scherer

Cornelsen

Cornelsen English Library

Verlagsredaktion
Dr. Blanca-Maria Rudhart

Umschlaggestaltung
Heike Börner, dia

Umschlag
Australia Post Australian Post
Corel Library

Illustration
Michael Fleischmann

Gestaltung & technische Umsetzung
Anna Bakalovic und Annika Preyhs, Berlin

Für die wertvollen Hinweise zum Manuskript danken wir
Meryyn Whittaker

www.cornelsen.de

1. Auflage, 2. Druck 2014

Alle Drucke dieser Auflage sind inhaltlich unverändert und können im Unterricht nebeneinander verwendet werden.

Druck: Offizin Andersen Nexö, Leipzig

ISBN 978-3-464-31168-4

Inhalt gedruckt auf säurefreiem Papier aus nachhaltiger Forstwirtschaft.

Contents

PROLOGUE

The stage is empty. A young man steps from the wings, rather shyly, and starts to read hesitantly from a manuscript.

HENRY This is my story. It starts in the year 1783. The conditions for poor people in Britain were terrible then: No work, no food. If you've never been hungry, you don't know what it means to go without food for days ... I was a young boy of 14, the oldest son of a family of seven kids. My father, John Cable, God rest his soul, was ...

A loud voice from the auditorium interrupts him.

DIRECTOR No, no, no! This won't do. You can't just stand there and go on talking.

The director comes onto the stage.

HENRY But it's my story. Every word of it is true.

DIRECTOR Sure, but your audience won't care. We've got to act it out. Let me see. *(He takes the manuscript away from Henry and has a look.)* Aha. That sounds like a great scene. You and your father went to a farm to steal some food for your family. So it's a dark night ... *(He makes a sign and the lights are turned off; he shouts:)* with a bit of moonlight! *(A yellow spotlight is turned on.)* Now let's have some stage props ... a bush to show we're in the countryside, yes, and the farmhouse is over there ... All right, I'll play your father's part, and you'll simply re-enact what happened. *(He takes some costumes out of a trunk.)* Put this on, it'll make you feel like the poor boy you were. *(They dress up in rags.)* Here we go.

SCENE 1 .... The Theft

Two dark figures come out of the wings.

FATHER *(whispering)* Quiet, stupid boy! If they notice we're here, we're as good as dead! Stay in the dark and don't step on any leaves!

HENRY *(scared)* Father! Don't you think their dog will warn them? I'm not sure if …

FATHER *(interrupts him)* Their dog is dead. He's no danger any more. And now shut up, boy, or they'll hear us!

Henry and his father move silently to the farm and enter it. After a while, Henry and his father come out of the house, their arms full of bread, meat and vegetables.

FATHER *(surprised)* I didn't think that it would be so easy! Did you see all that food? We poor people starve and these rich farmers have larders full of food!

HENRY *(happy)* I'm so hungry I could have eaten all the food in that larder! Look at this bread and meat! Mum will be so happy! *Suddenly there are shouts in the background:* ALARM! STOP THIEF!

FATHER *(horrified)* Oh my God! Run and hide, boy! If they catch us … they'll hang us!

People rush onto the stage, seizing Henry who is loaded down with his stolen goods.

HENRY *(in panic)* They've got me!

His father gives himself up.

FARMER *(loud, angry)* Got you, you bloody thieves! Hold that boy – he's wild! Don't move or you'll get a bash on your head! *(Father and son are led off the stage.)*

SCENE 2 .... A Heavy Sentence

COURT USHER Silence in the courtroom. *(The judge appears. Everyone stands up.)*

JUDGE The court is in session. *(Henry and his father are led in.)*

COURT USHER Your Lordship! John Cable and his son Henry. They were caught stealing food from Mr Benton's farm.

JUDGE John Cable? This is not the first time you have appeared in court, but it will certainly be the last. You dirty thief! This time you'll be hanged. It's the only way to keep you from stealing other people's property. *(There is some commotion in the courtroom. The judge bangs his gavel.)* Quiet, everybody! And that boy is following right in his father's footsteps. The best thing will be to hang him, too!

HENRY'S MOTHER Please have mercy, Your Lordship! My son is only 14. He still has his whole life before him. Please, don't let him hang! He is too young to die.

JUDGE Well, he is not too young to steal, is he? Hang a thief when he's young, and he'll no' steal when he's old.

HENRY'S FATHER We have no food! Poverty is not a crime.

JUDGE Quiet, thief! Is that what you teach your children: Steal whatever you need? I'm here to punish your crimes. Your son will go to prison – 14 years of hard labour will teach him that crime doesn't pay! Take him to jail! The court is adjourned. *(He raps his gavel. Henry's mother bursts into tears. Her son and husband are led away.)*

SCENE 3 .... In Prison

Henry is thrown into prison. Several convicts are lying on the floor.

CONVICT A Welcome to jail, son. What brought you here?

HENRY Me and my father stole some food. My father was hanged. They let me get away with 14 years.

CONVICT B Hanged, you say? Ha, that's what the government does for the poor: hang them! If they put us in prison, they still have to feed us, you know.

CONVICT A Feed us? What we get to eat in here can't be called "food". A rat wouldn't touch it!

A warden appears with a huge pot of gruel and hands out their rations.

HENRY *(tasting the gruel)* Yecch!

CONVICT A AND B Ha, ha, you'll get used to it. Hunger is the best sauce.

CONVICT C *(banging his wooden bowl and loudly singing)* Rule Britannia, Britannia rule the waves; Britons never-never-never shall be slaves! Hooray!

HENRY What's wrong with him?

CONVICT B That poor guy went mad. He's been here for over ten years, you know.

GUARD *(shouts)* Lunchtime is over. Time to get back to work.

THE CONVICTS' SONG
(Tune: What shall we do with a drunken sailor?)

What will you do with us convicts, jailer?
What will you do with us convicts, jailer?
What will you do with us convicts, jailer –
daily without warning?

Lock us and mock us and threaten to sock us –
that's what you'll do with us convicts, jailer,
that's what you'll do with us convicts,
jailer –
daily without warning!

Strip us and clip us and brutally whip us –
that's *(etc.)*

Beat us and cheat us and badly mistreat us –
(etc.)

Hooray! What great surprises
Hooray! What great surprises
Hooray! What great surprises,
daily without warning!

HENRY *(as the narrator)* That was my first day in prison. After three years in that world of hardship and terror, when I had just turned 17, the greatest event in my life as a convict took place. I was then working in the canteen …

SCENE 4 .... Henry Meets Susannah

SUSANNAH *(carrying something heavy, she stumbles and falls)* Aargh!

HENRY Let me help you. This is much too heavy for you.

GUARD Hey, you! That's her job, not yours!

HENRY Can't you see that she's only a young girl? She hasn't got enough strength for the job. How can you be so heartless? *(The guard turns away. Henry helps Susannah.)*

SUSANNAH Thank you. That was very kind of you.

HENRY Don't mention it. We've all got to help each other.

SUSANNAH You are very brave to talk to a guard like that.

HENRY Well, I was angry about the way he treated you.

SUSANNAH Oh, I'm used to being treated like that. Even my parents were always shouting at me.

HENRY I could never shout at you. You've got the prettiest face I've ever seen.

SUSANNAH I've heard that kind of talk before.

HENRY But I am serious. *(holding out his hand)* My name is Henry.

SUSANNAH I'm Susannah. I've been here for three months. Stole some silver spoons from my mistress. She had so many of them, I thought she wouldn't notice. But she did.

HENRY The rich always notice when the poor take something away from them. That's the only time when they notice the poor at all. *(They sit down together.)*

SUSANNAH You are right. I worked hard for my masters, but they treated me like dirt. "You should be glad to be a serving girl," they used to tell me. "Some poor girls are out in the street, with no job at all." Most of the time I went hungry and I had hardly any clothing to keep off the cold. *(They share some bread from his pocket. The guard shouts.)*

HENRY *(as the narrator, front stage)* Do I have to tell you that I had fallen in love with Susannah? She was the most beautiful girl I had ever seen – to be sure, I had not seen too many girls in prison. At any rate, we took to liking each other so much that we wanted to get married. But alas! That was not possible in prison. Yet even without a wedding we got a child. No, – not the two of us. One of the female convicts died in childbirth, and Susannah and I decided to bring up her poor baby ... *(A baby screams. Enter Susannah with the child, singing a lullaby.)*

SCENE 5 .... A Baby for the Colonies?

SUSANNAH'S LULLABY

Hush, little baby, don't say a word,
Papa's going to buy you a mocking bird.

If the mocking bird won't sing,
Papa's going to buy you a diamond ring.

If the diamond ring turns to brass,
Papa's going to buy you a looking-glass.

If the looking-glass gets broke,

Papa's going to buy you a billy-goat.

If that billy-goat runs away,
Papa's going to buy you another today.

SUSANNAH *(holding the baby in her arms)* Isn't he sweet?

HENRY Yes, indeed.

SUSANNAH Poor darling! To be born in prison!

HENRY But he won't grow up in here. Listen: There's talk that a number of convicts will be sent to the colonies ... *(Other convicts gather around them.)*

CONVICT A The colonies? Britain has lost her overseas colonies. The Americans won independence from the crown, God bless them!

CONVICT B Henry doesn't mean America – he's talking about Australia!

CONVICT A Australia? Where's that?

CONVICT B Down under. On the other side of the globe. On the far side of beyond, you know.

CONVICT A And why would they want to send us there?

CONVICT B It's an easy way to get rid of us. The prisons are overcrowded with all the poor. If you can't hang them all, send them to the colonies!

CONVICT C Rule Britannia, Britannia rule the wav...

ALL Oh, shut up!

GUARD Quiet everybody! *(The prisoners are huddled together, looking rather apprehensive.)* I've got a list of all the convicts who will be taken to Australia. Rebecca Knowles! *(She moves up to him. The others are not sure if they should envy her or feel sorry for her.)* Sarah Parker! Susannah

Wilson! *(Susannah holds on to Henry.)* Come on, girl, what's the matter?

HENRY I'll go with her! I love her, and we want to get married.

GUARD Forget it! There are only women on my list. You'll have to stay here.

HENRY But we're both taking care of the child! Let me go with them … please, let me go with them.

GUARD You don't understand. I'm under orders. She must go and you must stay here. There is nothing I can do for you.

HENRY Look, we …

GUARD That's enough. I've got to do my job. *(To his fellow officer)* Take them away.

SUSANNAH Henry! *(She is led away; Henry is held back by the guard.)*

HENRY I love you, Susannah. We'll see each other again, I promise.

HENRY *(as the narrator, frontstage)* Maybe it was foolish to promise "We'll see each other again". After all, Australia was far away and I was in prison with eleven years to go. But in the end …

The DIRECTOR dressing up as CAPTAIN motions him to be quiet and sends him off the stage. In the meantime a "ship" has been set up with a gangway. A ship's horn hoots. The CAPTAIN takes his position on board; the GUARD brings up the female convicts. Susannah is first on the gangway.

CAPTAIN What's this? I have no order to take babies! Take it away from her!

SUSANNAH — No, you can't! I'm minding him. My little one! *(crying)*

CAPTAIN — I'm under orders. I can't take babies. This is not a family outing, you understand.

GUARD — The baby was born in Norwich Jail, and this woman's name is on my list.

CAPTAIN — Well, the woman can stay, but the baby will have to go straight back to Norwich Jail. Take him away. I've got to do my job.

SUSANNAH — My darling! Don't take him away from me! You took away my dearest friend, but don't take away the little one! Who will take care of him?

GUARD — Listen. I know this is not my job, but … Give me the baby and I'll try to get some help for you. *(He takes her aside and talks quietly to her. She resigns and hands him her baby. Meanwhile the stage has been set for the next scene.)*

SCENE 6 ……. Lady Sydney

The Lady is sitting at her dressing table. Her maid is doing up her Ladyship's hair.

LADY SYDNEY — Is my husband in, Julia?

JULIA — No, your Ladyship. He went to Downing Street to see the Prime Minister.

LADY SYDNEY — Ah, they'll probably be discussing the deportation of convicts to that new continent.

JULIA — Excuse me for saying so, your Ladyship, but I'd rather be hanged than go to a place unknown. Home is home though it's never so homely, as the proverb says.

LADY SYDNEY You can't call prison a home, Julia.

JULIA Certainly not, your Ladyship. But better the devil you know than the devil you don't know.

LADY SYDNEY My dear Julia, there's another proverb that says "Of two evils choose the lesser." I believe that sending those poor people to Australia might offer them an opportunity to start a new life. *(Enter a servant)* Yes?

SERVANT There's a man from Norwich Jail who wants to see you, your Ladyship. He says it's very important.

LADY SYDNEY Norwich Jail? Didn't my husband arrange for female convicts from that terrible place to go to the new colony of Australia? Show him in.

GUARD Good morning, your Ladyship. My name is Harold Thompson. I'm a guard at Norwich Jail. This baby here ...

LADY SYDNEY He looks sweet.

GUARD He was born in prison, your Ladyship. Two young convicts have adopted him. I don't know about their crimes, but I can assure you that they really love each other and treat the baby like it was their own.

LADY SYDNEY So – what can I do for them?

GUARD They wanted to get married. Now the mother is being sent to Australia, without the support of that young man – and without the baby!

LADY SYDNEY That's horrible! We should stop treating these people like animals and start treating them like human beings.

GUARD That's how I feel, too. But only what you say will make a difference, your Ladyship.

LADY SYDNEY Well, I say that it's a shame and a disgrace. Why should this poor little thing have to suffer? Whatever wrong those young people have done, let's give them another chance.

GUARD You are very kind, your Ladyship.

LADY SYDNEY In Australia the convicts will be able to make a fresh start. They'll get a piece of land to feed themselves. Those two young people – what are their names? *(She sits down at her writing desk, and dismisses her maid.)*

GUARD Henry Cable and Susannah Wilson, your Ladyship.

LADY SYDNEY Well, Henry and Susannah will have my permission to get married as soon as they touch the coast of the new continent. *(She writes something on a piece of paper.)* Take this to the captain.

GUARD Thank you, your Ladyship.

LADY SYDNEY Erm, by the way: Who sent you here?

GUARD People told me that you are in charge of …

LADY SYDNEY True, but taking care of babies is not your job, is it?

GUARD No, your Ladyship.

LADY SYDNEY So you didn't carry out anyone's orders?

GUARD Not this time, your Ladyship. I only looked at the baby and … and …

LADY SYDNEY I see. Sometimes you have to listen to what your heart tells you to do. You are a good man. Too many people don't bother to listen to their hearts. Or maybe their hearts have stopped talking. Now go and rescue those poor young people. *(The guard bows and leaves. She calls her maid)* Julia? Julia! *(Exit Lady Sydney.)*

SCENE 7 .... Marriage on the Beach

The sounds of birds and animals of the forest, and the didgeridoo in the distance – the melody of a new continent. Henry and Susannah appear on the stage. They are tired but happy.

HENRY We've finally reached our destination.

SUSANNAH After seven months on board that terrible ship. I can't believe that we're still alive. But we made it – the three of us, praised be the Lord.

HENRY *(looking around in wonder)* Isn't this a fantastic place?

SUSANNAH I don't know. It's so different from our home country.

HENRY Our home country only meant prison to us. And all we could look forward to was starvation. Trust me: We'll make this our new home.

SUSANNAH Our first home. This is a new beginning. For us and for this child.

They wander off the stage. Other travellers appear.

CAPTAIN *(in his dress uniform, glass in hand)* Pooh! It's awfully hot. Just imagine: This is January 26. In England people are sitting at the fireside looking out through frost-covered windows at the snow. We'll celebrate next Christmas in the summer!

PARSON True. Everything seems to be the other way round on this side of the globe. But why think of Christmas? Our first celebration was raising the Union flag and toasting the king. And the second one is going to be a wedding.

CAPTAIN You mean Henry and Susannah, those two convicts who got on board together, with Lady Sydney's permission?

PARSON Yes, today the two young people will at last get married.

CAPTAIN They had to travel all around the globe for this!

PARSON "The ways of our Lord are wonderful."

CAPTAIN Yes, Lord Sydney is a wonderful man – especially with Lady Sydney behind him.

Preparations are made. An altar is set up, flowers are placed on and around it. All the convicts have put on clean clothes.

PARSON Dearly beloved, we are gathered together in a spirit of joy and thankfulness. The Lord has led us to this new shore. And this beautiful morning tells us the good tidings of a new beginning. It tells you to leave your sorrows and your sins behind you and to start afresh. Let us all share this spirit of hope and conciliation. There are two among your number who are chosen to be symbols of this new promise: Henry and Susannah will join their hands and their hearts in the sight of God, and in the face of this congregation.

The wedding march.
Henry and Susannah appear, dressed in their finest. A friend carries their little child in her arms.

PARSON Wilt thou, Henry Cable, have this woman, Susannah Wilson, to thy wedded wife? Wilt thou love her, comfort her, honour, and keep her in sickness and in health, so long as ye both shall live?

HENRY I will.

PARSON Wilt thou, Susannah Wilson, have this man, Henry Cable, to thy wedded husband? Wilt thou obey him, and serve him, love, honour, and keep him in sickness and in health, so long as ye both shall live?

SUSANNAH I will.

PARSON You may kiss the bride.

CAPTAIN And this is my wedding present for you: You have both been pardoned by the King. From now on, you are free people and you may settle on a piece of land of your own choice.

THE MAD CONVICT Rule Britannia, Britannia rule the waves … *(Singing on he throws rice about.)*

EVERYBODY Hooray! *(Music)*

SONG: BOTANY BAY
(Traditional)

Farewell to old England forever,
Farewell to my rum culls as well;
Farewell to the well-known old Bailee,
Where I used to cut such a swell.

Chorus
Singing too-ral li-ooral li-ad-dity
Singing too-ral li-ooral li-ay;
Singing too-ral li-ooral li-ad-dity
Singing too-ral li-ooral li-ay.

'Taint leaving old England we cares about,
'Taint cos we mispels what we knows,
But becos all we light-fingered gentry
Hops around with a log on our toes.

Chorus
Singing too-ral li-ooral li-ad-dity …

For seven long years I'll be staying here,
For seven long years and a day,
For meeting a cove in an area
And taking his ticker away.

Chorus
Singing too-ral li-ooral li-ad-dity …

Now, all my young Dookies and Duchesses,
Take warning from what I've to say,
Mind all is your own as you touchesses,
Or you'll find us in Botany Bay.

Chorus
Singing too-ral li-ooral li-ad-dity …

HENRY *(front stage):* We had reached a new shore in every sense of the word. Yet our troubles were far from over. We had a lucky break, but it turned out to be only – a break!

INTERMISSION

SCENE 8 .... Meeting the Natives

HENRY When we came to Australia, we thought it was an empty country only waiting for us to settle in it. How wrong we were! People had been living there for a long, long time. At first we called them "Indians".

DIRECTOR Indians, eh? Well, I've got a surprise for you!

Actors dressed up as "Indians" appear on stage, doing a "war dance".

HENRY No, no, you've got it all wrong – not American Indians, Australian Indians, Aborigines, you know. They walked about naked, with their bodies and faces painted.

DIRECTOR Naked? I'm not sure the audience will accept that.

HENRY Well, let them put on black underwear.

DIRECTOR We'll see about that. At least I hope your story can do without those hopping animals – kangaroos I believe they're called. *(exit)*

Henry's and Susannah's lodge: a piece of canvas stretched over a couple of poles. Henry is cutting wood. Susannah is sewing a child's dress.

HENRY Goodness, this wood is terribly hard! I'm working like a slave, although I'm a free man now. *(He sits down to take a rest.)*

SUSANNAH Just keep in mind: We're free at last and we've got a piece of land to live on. Ah, it's too good to be true.

HENRY Sure, but there's a lot of work ahead of us. Food doesn't grow by itself, you know!

SUSANNAH I certainly do. Or do you think I'm sitting around twiddling my thumbs?

A small group of aborigines appear. Henry holds his axe like a weapon, ready to defend himself.

HENRY What do they want? I don't like the look of this.

SUSANNAH We met one of them before, down in the army camp – remember?

HENRY Yes. Bennelong – wasn't that his name? And he can speak our language. Hi Benny, what are you up to?

BEN Hi. This is your place?

HENRY Yes. How do you like it?

BEN Not much. It's in the way.

HENRY In the way? In the way of what, may I ask?

BEN This is our road. Very old road.

HENRY A road? You must be kidding. I can't see a road anywhere around. The only road in this country is the one they are building from Botany Bay to Sydney.

BEN We travel here. On our road.

HENRY I don't mind if you travel here. Just make sure to walk around my place, that's all.

BEN We walk here.

HENRY Don't be ridiculous. This is a big country. You can walk anywhere you like. But this is my land. *(to Susannah)* What can I do about these pig-headed natives?

Bennelong translates to the others. They react angrily.

BEN Land doesn't belong to anybody. We only walk through it.

HENRY Go ahead and walk – as long as you keep on the other side of my fence.

BEN You don't understand. We must have our road. It's the road of our forefathers, the road of our dreams.

HENRY Your dreams? And what about our dreams? Do you know what we went through before we got here? This is our place. This is the place of our dreams.

Bennelong turns away sadly to the others. He translates briefly what Henry told him. They make threatening gestures, but finally move away.

HENRY Phew! I'm glad they're gone.

SUSANNAH But they might come back – in larger numbers!

HENRY We'll have to be watchful.

(as the narrator, front stage) We were really worried. There had been some clashes between natives and white settlers, from the very first days of the colony, and some white people had got injured or killed – and many natives, too. To my wife and me it meant nights of broken sleep …

SCENE 9 .... A Terrible Night

The stage is dark. There is a thunderstorm, with flashes of light and peals of thunder. Sounds of the didgeridoo, drums and chanting, which gradually become louder. Masked dancers appear while Henry and his wife are sleeping in their shelter, both of them restless. The dance is a nightmare, not reality. When the native music is at its loudest, it suddenly stops. The dancers disappear. Silence. A dark figure appears and prowls around the place. When he opens the larder, there is a noise.

HENRY *(starts and shouts)* Who's there?

The figure takes some food out of the larder and tries to sneak away with it. Henry fires a shot at the thief. The figure falls to the ground, moaning.

SUSANNAH What's happening?

HENRY I just shot a thief.

SUSANNAH Oh dear. I hope you didn't kill him.

HENRY I don't care. He tried to steal our food.

They move to the figure on the ground, holding a lantern.

SUSANNAH Oh my God! It's Bennelong!

HENRY So what? All those natives are the same. They walk around the country and they take what they can get. I don't mind – as long as they don't take what belongs to me!

Susannah has taken a closer look at the wounded native.

SUSANNAH It's his leg. Your bullet broke his bone.

HENRY Should I have let him run away? He's a thief, isn't he?

SUSANNAH Isn't that what brought us here? You've come a long way, Henry.

They look at each other in silence. Bennelong moans.

HENRY Do you – do you think he'll live?

SUSANNAH Yes, if we take good care of him. Help me to set the bone.

HENRY *(as the narrator, front stage)* We managed to heal Ben's leg. He stayed with us for a couple of weeks. Of course, we had to feed him during this time. He used up more food this way than he could have stolen that night.

But somehow I was glad that he lived. I couldn't help thinking of my father, poor man. Poverty had killed him, and now it had nearly made me a killer.

DIRECTOR Well, so the man survived. And did you have any more problems with the natives after that?

HENRY There was a much bigger problem we had to face: the drought.

SCENE 10 .... A Neighbour's Call

A neighbouring farmer and his wife, Will and Jane Swift, are paying a visit.

WILL G'day, Henry. G'day, Sue.

They greet each other.

JANE Pooh, this heat just doesn't let up. How's your corn?

SUSANNAH Not too bad. But if we don't get any rain soon, it'll dry up.

WILL This is a hard country.

They eat biscuits and drink tea.

SUSANNAH How do you like my biscuits?

JANE *(crunching on one)* Mmmh. Very nice.

WILL I hear that you had some trouble with the natives?

HENRY Y-yes.

WILL Is it true that you kept one of them on your place after you shot him?

HENRY Uh-huh.

WILL *(shaking his head)* I don't get it. All I can say is: Shoot the bastards whenever they start making trouble. They're a pack of no-good thieves.

JANE All they do is lie naked in the shade all day long.

WILL And come night, they're off stealing.

SUSANNAH But some are different.

WILL AND JANE *(surprised)* What?

SUSANNAH Take Benny – that's Bennelong – for example. He has offered to help us on the farm.

WILL Help you? Can you imagine a native doing farm work, eh, Jane?

JANE I employed one of those black girls in the house for a while. O my! All she did was steal sugar. *(She takes a couple of spoonfuls from the sugar bowl to put in her cup.)* I can do without that kind of help, thank you.

WILL The convicts – excuse me, Henry, you used to be one of them, too – the convicts, I say, make better farm workers, all in all.

HENRY Well, I'll give Benny a chance. If we can't get any water soon, we'll be finished anyway.

They are all silent for a while.

WILL Thanks for the tea. We'd better be going.

JANE Let's hope for rain. I wish they could send us some over from England ...

WILL ... but all they do is send over more people.

JANE And some of the first settlers are already talking of going back home.

SUSANNAH Are you among those?

They stand around awkwardly.

WILL We've given it some thought.

JANE If there's no change of weather, we'll pack our things and take the first ship back.

HENRY We're staying – if only because we can't pay for the passage to England.

They say their good-byes silently.

DIRECTOR What is this leading to? I thought you had become a successful settler in Australia and wanted to show your countrymen the road to a better life.

HENRY I'm only telling my story. And I've still got to tell the ending. Then you can let the audience decide if it's only one man's story or a new turn of history.

DIRECTOR The ending? A happy one, I presume?

HENRY Wait and see. Things looked pretty bad for us. The rain wouldn't come. The river ran dry. The plants turned brown and the cattle were dying of thirst. Now this is what happened. *(He hands the last pages of his manuscript to the director – who has a look at them, then exits.)*

SCENE 11 ……. Saved!

The parson is paying a call.

PARSON Ah, it's certainly hard times. You haven't been spared much in life.

SUSANNAH Oh yes, vicar. We can't take it much longer, I'm afraid. There's hardly any water left for us, let alone the animals.

PARSON I know, but what can I do? Believe me, I've been praying for rain day and night.

HENRY It hasn't helped much, has it?

SUSANNAH Some of our prayers have been answered, don't forget.

The natives appear, led by Bennelong.

HENRY Uh-oh, more trouble.

BEN I've come to say good-bye to you.

HENRY I'm sorry you're leaving. *(They shake hands.)* The way it looks, we might be leaving soon, too.

SUSANNAH At least you have a place to go to.

BEN This was our place before you came. But I don't want you to die here. You helped me – I help you.

The natives hand them a water jar.

SUSANNAH Erm, thanks.

HENRY We appreciate this, but we'd really need much more water, you know – for the fields and the animals.

BEN There is more of this – here on your land.

HENRY AND SUSANNAH What?

BEN We know where a spring is. It's not far. We'll show you.

HENRY You mean: we've got our own water reservoir? Right in our backyard? *(Henry exits with the natives.)*

SUSANNAH This is too good to be true.

PARSON The Lord provides. Only trust in him.

SUSANNAH Isn't it amazing how much these people know? When I came here, I didn't think very highly of the natives. I've changed my mind.

PARSON They might be clever in their own way, but on the whole, they're like children. "Theirs is the Kingdom of Heaven".

SUSANNAH Heaven is about the only place left to them after we've taken over their land.

HENRY *(coming back enthusiastically)* It's true! We've got a well on our land. There'll be plenty of water! *(Henry and Susannah do a little jig, singing)* The drought is over, oh what fun, oh what fun, all our trouble's gone!

PARSON You're saved, thank the Lord.

HENRY Let's thank Benny first. Where is he?

SUSANNAH He's gone. He and his people are gone.

PARSON *(who pays no attention)* What a great blessing this is! Hallelujah!

DIRECTOR *(returns from the wings, the last pages of Henry's manuscript in hand)* So you really made it? You're a rich man with 1,000 sheep and 10 acres of corn! And there is still more good farmland to be had down under? Cheaply, too? *(He looks at the manuscript.)* Only £100 for a good-sized piece of farmland, you say? *(He puts on his coat and hat.)* I won't invest money in a production of your play if it's so easy to get rich as a farmer down under. Australia, here I come! *(He rushes off the stage.)*

HENRY Hey, what about my story?

DIRECTOR It's been a great success with me. As for the audience – find out for yourself! *(exit)*

HENRY *(stands flabbergasted)* What do you say to that?

The pianist strikes up a few chords of "Rule Britannia".

CURTAIN

Vocabulary

Abbreviations:
sb. = somebody
sth.= something
etw. = etwas
jmd. = jemand, jmdm. = jemandem
umgs. = umgangssprachlich

A

adjourned [ə'dʒɜnd] (Gerichtssitzung) unterbrochen
alas! [ə'læs] ach!
altar ['ɔːltə] Altar *(Aussprache beachten!)*
amazing [ə'meɪzɪŋ] verblüffend
(to) **appreciate** [ə'priːʃieɪt] schätzen, dankbar sein
apprehensive ['æprɪ'hensɪv] ängstlich, besorgt
at any rate [ət 'eni reɪt] auf jeden Fall
auditorium [ˌɔːdɪ'tɔːriəm] Zuschauerraum
awkwardly ['ɔːkwədli] verlegen, betreten
axe [æks] Axt

B

backyard ['bæk'jaːd], **in one's backyard** im eigenen Hinterhof
bash [bæʃ] Hieb
(be)cos = because
Better the devil you know than the devil you don't know ['betə ðə 'devl] *entspricht dem deutschen Sprichwort „Lieber den Spatz in der Hand als die Taube auf dem Dach"*
billy-goat ['bɪligəʊt] Ziegenbock
blessing ['blesɪŋ] Segen
(to) **bother** ['bɒðə(r)] sich Sorgen machen
(to) **bow** [baʊ] sich verbeugen
bowl [beʊl] Schüssel
brass [braːs] Messing
briefly ['briːfli] knapp
brutal ['bruːtl] brutal *(Aussprache beachten!)*
bullet ['bʊlɪt] Kugel
(to) **burst into tears** [bɜːst 'ɪntə tɪəs] in Tränen ausbrechen

C

canvas ['kænvəs] Stoff
(to) **carry out (orders)** ['kæri aʊt] (Befehle) ausführen
(to) **chant** [tʃaːnt] singen (Ritual)
(to be) **in charge of** [ɪn 'tʃadʒ əv] das Sagen haben, die Verantwortung tragen
(to) **cheat** [tʃiːt] betrügen
clash [klæʃ] Zusammenstoß, Auseinandersetzung
(to) **clip** [klɪp] *(umgs.)* ohrfeigen

come night [kʌm 'naɪt] sobald es Nacht wird
(to) **comfort** sb. ['kʌmfət] jmd. trösten
commotion [kə'məʊʃn] Aufregung
conciliation [kənˌsɪli'eɪʃn] Versöhnung
convict ['kɒnvɪkt] Sträfling
courtroom ['kɔ:tru:m] Gerichtssaal
cove [kəʊv] *(veraltet)* Kerl, Typ
(to) **crunch** [krʌntʃ] knabbern
(to) **cut such a swell** [ˌkʌt sʌtʃ‿ə‿'swel] *(umgs.)* sich wie ein feiner Herr aufführen

D

destination [ˌdestɪ'neɪʃn] Ziel, Bestimmung
didgeridoo [ˌdɪdʒəri'du] *Blasinstrument der australischen Ureinwohner*
disgrace [dɪs'greɪs] Schande, Schandfleck
(to) **dismiss** [dɪs'mɪs] entlassen
don't mention it [dəʊnt 'menʃn ɪt] nicht der Rede wert
Dookie = Duke ['du:ki] Herzog (*weibl. Form:* Duchess)
down under [daʊn 'ʌndə] *(scherzhaft für)* Australien
Downing Street ['daʊnɪŋ stri:t] *Amtssitz des britischen Premierministers*
dress uniform [dres 'ju:nɪfɔ:m] Galauniform
(to be) **dressed in their finest** [drest ɪn ðeə(r) 'faɪnɪst] in Sonntagskleidern
dressing table [ˌdresɪŋ 'teɪbl] Frisiertisch

E

(to) **employ** sb. [ɪm'plɔɪ] jmd. anstellen
(to) **envy** ['envɪ] beneiden

F

(to) **face** sth. [feɪs] (einem Problem) ins Auge blicken
fellow (officer) ['feləʊ 'ɒfɪsə] Kollege, Kamerad
(to) **fend off** ['fend ɒf] abhalten
flabbergasted ['flæbəga:stɪd] verblüfft
flash of light [flæʃ əv laɪt] aufzuckendes Licht
forefathers ['fɔ:fa:ðəz] Vorfahren, Ahnen

G

gangway ['gæŋweɪ] Planke
gavel ['gævl] (Holz-)Hammer *(für den Richter)*
gestures ['dʒestʃəz] Gesten
get broke = break
God bless [gɒd bles] Gott segne
God rest his soul [ˌgɒd rest hɪz 'səʊl] Gott sei seiner Seele gnädig
good tidings [gʊd 'taɪdɪŋz] frohe Botschaft
good-sized [ˌgʊd'saɪzd] ziemlich groß
gradually ['grædʒuəli] nach und nach
(to) **greet** [gri:t] (be)grüßen
gruel ['gru:əl] Haferschleim
guy [gaɪ] Kerl, Typ

H

hard labour [hɑːd ˈleɪbə] Zwangsarbeit

(to) **have mercy** [ˈmɜːsi] Erbarmen haben

heartless [ˈhɑːtləs] herzlos

heaven [ˈhevn] Himmel

hesitant [ˈhezɪtənt] zögernd

homely [ˈhəʊmli] heimelig, behaglich

(to) **honour** sb. [ˈɒnə(r)] jmd. respektieren, achten

(to) **hoot** [huːt] (Signalhorn) heulen, pfeifen

(to) **hop around with a log on our toes** [hɒp əˈraʊnd wið ə lɒg ɒn aː təʊz] mit einem Holzklotz am Bein (*toe:* Zeh) herumhüpfen

(to be) **horrified** [ˈhɒrɪfaɪd] entsetzt

(to be) **huddled together** [ˈhʌdld təˈgeðə] aneinander gekauert

human being [ˈhjuːmən ˈbiːɪŋ] menschliches Wesen, Mensch

Hunger is the best sauce [ˈhʌŋgər ɪz ðə best sɔːs] Hunger ist der beste Koch. *(Sprichwort)*

hush [hʌʃ] still!

I

Indians [ˈindiənz] *urspr. Inder; nach der Entdeckung Amerikas (= „Indien") Bezeichnung für die dortigen Ureinwohner (dt. „Indianer") und für weitere Ureinwohner unbekannter Regionen, wie z. B. Australien*

J

jail [dʒeɪl] Gefängnis

jailer [ˈdʒeɪlə(r)] Gefängniswärter

jig [dʒɪg] Freudentanz

joy [dʒɔɪ] Freude

K

(to) **keep in mind** [kiːp ɪn maɪnd] daran denken

(to be) **kidding** [ˈkɪdɪŋ] Spaß machen, scherzen

knee [niː] Knie

L

lantern [ˈlæntən] Laterne

larder [ˈlaːdə] Speisekammer

let alone [let əˈləʊn] ganz zu schweigen von

light-fingered gentry [ˌlaɪtˈfɪngəd ˈdʒentri] „langfingrige Gesellschaft"

lodge [lɒdʒ] Hütte

looking-glass [ˈlʊkɪŋglaːs] Spiegel

lullaby [ˈlʌləbaɪ] Wiegenlied

M

maid [meɪd] Zofe

(to) **mistreat** [ˌmɪsˈtriːt] misshandeln

mistress/master [ˈmɪstrəs| ˈmaːstə(r)] Herrin/Herr

(to) **moan** [məʊn] stöhnen

(to) **mock** [mɒk] veralbern

(to) **motion** sb. **to do** sth. [ˈməʊʃn] jmd. ein Zeichen geben, dass er etw. tun soll

N

(to be) **naked** [ˈneɪkɪd] nackt

new turn of history [ə njuː tɜːn‿əv ˈhɪstri] ein neuer Zeitbeginn

a **no-good** [ə ˈnəʊgʊd] Taugenichts

O

(to) **obey** [ə'beɪ] gehorchen
Old Bailee = Old Bailey [ˌəʊld 'beɪli] *bekanntes Gerichtsgebäude in London*
opportunity [ˌɒpə'tju:nəti] Gelegenheit, Chance
outing ['aʊtɪŋ] Ausflug
(to be) **overcrowded** [ˌəʊvə'kraʊdɪd] überfüllt, übervölkert

P

(to be) **pardoned** ['pa:dnd] begnadigt werden
parson ['pa:sn] Pfarrer
(to) **pay a call** [peɪ ə kɔ:l] *(förmlich)* einen Besuch machen
a peal of thunder [ə ˌpi:l əv 'θʌndə] Donnergrollen
permission [pə'mɪʃn] Erlaubnis
pigheaded [pɪg'hedɪd] störrisch
(to) **place** [pleɪs] stellen, legen
praised be the Lord [preɪzd bi: ðə lɔ:d] dem Herrn sei Dank
(to) **presume** [prɪ'zju:m] vermuten
proverb ['prɒvɜ:b] Sprichwort
(to) **provide** [prə'vaɪd] sorgen für
(to) **prowl** [praʊl] herumstöbern

R

rags [rægz] Lumpen
rap/bang the gavel [ˌræp ðə 'gævl] mit dem Hammer (des Vorsitzenden) klopfen
rat [ræt] Ratte
ration ['ræʃn] Ration
(to) **re-enact** [ˌri:ɪ'nækt] (Szene) nachspielen
(to) **resign** [rɪ'zaɪn] aufgeben
restless ['restləs] unruhig
ridiculous [rɪ'dɪkjəles] lächerlich
Rule Britannia [ˌru:l brɪ'tænjə] *inoffizielle Nationalhymne, komponiert von Thomas Augustine Arne (um 1740) zu einem Gedicht von James Thomson (1700 – 1748)*
rum culls [rʌm kʌlz] „Saufbrüder"
(to) **run dry** [rʌn draɪ] austrocknen
(to) **rush off** [rʌʃ 'ɒf] wegeilen, fortstürzen

S

(to be) **in session** [ɪn 'seʃn] eine Sitzung abhalten, tagen
(to) **set the bone** [ˌset ðə 'bəʊn] den Knochen richten, schienen
(to) **set the stage** [set ðə steɪdʒ] die Bühne herrichten
(to) **settle** ['setl] (be)siedeln
shade [ʃeɪd] Schatten
shame [ʃeɪm] Schande
shore [ʃɔ:] Küste, Strand
silent ['saɪlənt] leise, still
sin [sɪn] Sünde
(to) **sneak away** [sni:k ə'weɪ] sich davonschleichen
(to) **sock** [sɒk] *(umgs.)* hauen
sorrows ['sɒrəʊz] Kummer
(to be) **spared** sth. [spɜəd] etw. nicht erleiden müssen
spirit ['spɪrɪt] Geist
spotlight ['spɒtlaɪt] Scheinwerfer
stage props ['steɪdʒ prɒps] Requisiten

(to) **start afresh** [ˌstaːt ə'freʃ] neu beginnen
strength [streŋθ] Stärke, Kraft
(to) **strike a few chords** [straɪk ə fjuː kɔːds] ein paar Akkorde anschlagen
(to) **strip** [strɪp] entkleiden
(to) **stumble** ['stʌmbl] stolpern

T

'taint [teɪnt] = it isn't
(to) **take it** ['teɪk ɪt] aushalten
(to) **take to liking** sb. [ˌteɪk tə 'laɪkɪŋ] jmd. lieb gewinnen
theft [θeft] Diebstahl
(to) **think highly of** sb. [θɪŋk 'haɪli əv] jmd. wertschätzen
this won't do [θɪs wəʊnt duː] so geht's nicht
threaten ['θretn] bedrohen
thunderstorm ['θʌndəstɔːm] Gewitter
ticker ['tɪkə] *(umgs.)* Uhr
(to) **toast** [təʊst] zuprosten
(to) **treat** [triːt] behandeln
trunk [trʌŋk] Truhe
(to) **trust in** sb. ['trʌst ɪn] jmdm. vertrauen
(to) **turn mad** [tɜːn mæd] verrückt werden
(to) **twiddle** one's **thumbs** ['twɪdl wʌnz θʌmz] Däumchen drehen

U

under orders ['ʌndər 'ɔːdəz] in Befehlsnotstand
underwear ['ʌndəweə(r)] Unterwäsche
Union flag [ˌjuːniən 'flæg] *Fahne des Vereinigten Königreichs*
(to be) **up to** sth. [ʌp tuː] etw. im Schilde führen
usher ['ʌʃə(r)] Gerichtsdiener

V

vicar ['vɪkə] Pfarrer

W

(to) **wander off** ['wɒndər ɒf] (langsam) weggehen
warden ['wɔːdn] Wärter
watchful ['wɒtʃfl] aufmerksam, umsichtig
we cares = we care
we mispels = we misspell [ˌmɪs'spelz] falsch schreiben
well [wel] Brunnen
(to) **whip** [wɪp] peitschen

Some notes on the play

FROM PRISON TO PROSPERITY evolved from a creative writing project in class 9. My students produced scenes ranging from the theft (at the beginning of the play) to the convicts' wedding on the Australian shore (before intermission), based on a story about Lord Sydney's penal colony in the 18th century. The scenes had to be elaborated on, to some extent, and a second part – set on the new continent – was added to create a full-length script. Interested students formed a drama group to produce the play. During the first rehearsals the script was still open to suggestions from the participants because I wanted to make sure that the text suited the speakers (i. e. their linguistic and acting skills) and that the drama was within their scope. The "world première" took place at the Europa-Gymnasium Wörth on June 24, 2004.

Tips for Performing the Play

A play can be fun to read – and this playlet is no exception, I hope –, without any obligation to put it on the stage. However, "the proof of the pudding is in the eating": The supreme test of a drama (and an extra boost to its appreciation) consists in staging it. As the director says in the prologue: "We've got to act it out." Of course, there are many steps between a staged reading and a full-fledged production of the play, but the shortness of the text, the absence of scenery and the adjustable size of the cast are calculated to facilitate a stage production.
Here are a few hints that might be of some help.

- THE STAGE: Speaking from personal experience, I recommend a bare stage for two reasons:

- The students should not rely on the scenery to create the atmosphere – it is rather their acting skills which are called for to convey the mood and the circumstances of the scene.
- The basic tenet of the play in hand is that it exists only as a manuscript which is to be turned into a stage production.
- The director/ producer/ stage manager uses all the stage props (and costumes) at his disposal, but keep in mind that the show is actually the first – and only! – rehearsal of the play.

- PROPS: When rehearsing the play, you will probably realize that a number of stage props and personal props are helpful. Why resort to mime play when all you need is some spoons and bowls to show convicts eating? In our production we used a box (1.50 x 0.70 x 0.50 m) as an all-purpose prop: "farmhouse" and larder, the judge's lectern, Lady Sydney's dressing table, the "ship" etc. The set was changed under the direction of the stage manager, with the curtain up all the time.
- THE NARRATOR: Henry is actually meant to be a middle-aged or even elderly person who gets cast as the youthful protagonist of his own biography. The story he is trying to tell (and, probably, to sell) is dramatized on the spot by the director, who takes on whatever part he thinks fit. Henry takes care not to lose the thread of his life story, and the director keeps the action going. In the end, the director exchanges the production of the play for the "reality" beyond the stage.
- COSTUMES: For the sake of historical verisimilitude, 18th century costumes should be used. However, apart from Lady Sydney's dress, there is no need for elaborate outfits. The

convicts go around in rags. Knee breeches, white shirts, and dark coats for Henry, the director, and the guards will do.

- CASTING: The play supplies a fairly large number of speaking and non-speaking parts. If need be, a class of 30 can be provided with roles; in my production a number of 11 students proved to be sufficient.
- MUSIC: Live music is, of course, recommendable. The piano, and the banjo (for the song "Botany Bay"), are the appropriate instruments. As it is difficult to find didgeridoo players in these parts, recordings of Aboriginal music must be used (e. g. by Yothu Yindi).
- SOUND AND LIGHT EFFECTS: I suggest using them sparingly. The nightmare (in scene 9), however, can be realized with a maximum of effect if, for instance, strobe lighting is used.

Some interesting facts

- The annual wage of a maidservant in 18th century England was £ 7.
- The favourite saying of the Scottish judge Robert MacQueen, Lord Braxfield (1722–99) was: "Hang a thief when he's young, and he'll no' steal when he's old".
- The First Fleet of eleven sailing-ships with 1,500 people including about 800 convicts left under Governor Philip in May 1787. They spent over eight months at sea and arrived at Botany Bay near Sydney in January 1788.
- Twenty-four of the 800 convicts on board six ships did not survive that voyage.
- Governor Phillip tried to establish friendly relationships with the Aborigines, but failed in the long run.
- An Aborigine named Bennelong visited England with Phillip in 1792 and stayed there for three years.
- Convicts in the Australian colonies were forced to walk 30 miles a day and carry 56 pounds.
- The transportation of convicts ended in 1857 after a total of 134,000 convicts had been sent to Australia.
- The didgeridoo of the Aborigines is a trumpet-like instrument which was originally made of a eucalyptus branch hollowed out by termites. It is usually 1–2½ m long and produces a large variety of humming and booming sounds. The musicians have developed the art of "circular breathing" (i. e. drawing breath and blowing into their instrument at the same time!). The didgeridoo is used for songs, dances, and healing ceremonies.
- 100 years after the first transport of convicts a law was passed (*Probation of First Offenders Act,* 1887) that ensured that petty

criminals under age were let off on probation. (In 1908 the *Children Act* finally prohibited the imprisonment of children under 14.)

Australia and Europe

When a map of Australia is put on one of a similar scale of Europe the size of Australia is easier to under-stand. Space and openness are two features that are special and important in Australia, especially in relationship to the relatively small population of 18,289,000 (June '96).

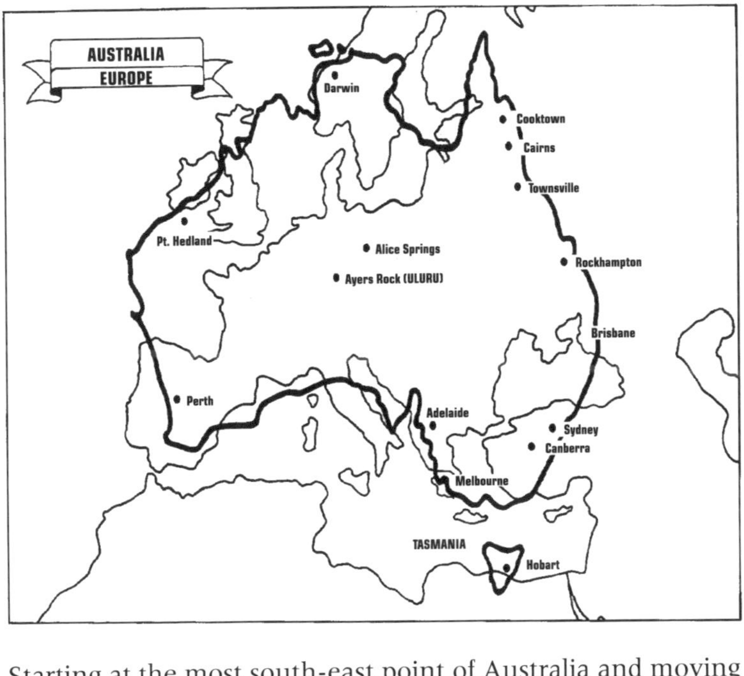

Starting at the most south-east point of Australia and moving anti-clockwise, Tasmania crosses the Mediterranean Sea and extends into Egypt, while Sydney to the north lies in central Turkey. The most north-east point of Australia, Cape York, is a third of the way along the border between Finland and Russia. The north coast of Australia then crosses central Sweden and

Norway, and goes down to the south-west to include Scotland and touches the coast of Ireland. The fifth continent's coast moves further west and then south through Portugal and includes most of Spain. Australia's long south coast starts with its most western part running through the Mediterranean Sea south of Spain and runs east enclosing most of Italy and Greece.
(from: Robyn Christensen *Australia & New Zealand A to Z*, Berlin 1998)

Further Reading

- Badger, Geoffrey, *Explorers of Australia* (Sydney: Kangaroo Press, 2001)
- Phillip, Captain Arthur, *Australien. Die Gründung einer Strafkolonie* (Göttingen: Lamuv, 2001)

Cornelsen Landeskunde Reader

- Christensen, Robyn, *Australia & New Zealand A to Z* (Bestellnr. 31888, ab 4. Lehrjahr)
- Dennis, Ann, *Spotlight on Australia* (Bestellnr. 100758, ab 5. Lehrjahr)
- Fenner, Patricia, *Down Under. Images of Australia* (Bestellnr. 51501, ab 5. Lehrjahr)
- Klewig, Bernd (Hrsg.), *The Australian Way – Tales from Down Under* (Bestellnr. 68455, ab 5. Lehrjahr)